The Survival Guide for Travelling with a Sensory Kiddo

Angie Voss, OTR/L

UnderstandingSPD.com

ISBN-13: 978-1468005813
ISBN-10: 1468005812

For my precious sensory kiddos
who were not able to find the joy and delight in
a trip to the beach or an amusement park.

CONTENTS

1 WHY IS TRAVELLING SO DIFFICULT?

Sensory kiddos love consistency, structure, and sameness. Their little world tends to be very scary, disorganized, and unpredictable...so routines and structure create a sense of comfort for the nervous system.

Actually, human beings in general like consistency, structure, and routine and often thrive in this type of environment. Think about the last time you slept in someone's guest room or in a hotel room. It was likely hard to fall asleep and get adjusted the first night. Or perhaps you woke up in the middle of the night and it took a moment to come to your senses and remember where you were.

These types of challenges which we face when we travel are magnified and **only that much more difficult for a sensory kiddo**.

Let's add to that the specific challenges that the child faces on a day to day basis even during their normal routine and environment. Possibly hyper-sensitive to sounds or touch, or crave and need constant movement or proprioception.

Now only imagine what even a weekend trip could do in regards to disruption of sensory processing. ☹

Research suggests that it takes at least THREE TIMES as long for a sensory child to adjust to the new surroundings as it does the child with a neuro-typical brain. And not only that, when the child returns home, it will take THREE TIMES as long to get adjusted back to the normal daily routine!

I think we can all somewhat understand this as well, since I know for myself it is hard to get back into the normal daily routine after even a weekend trip, and even that much more difficult after a week or two vacation.

Unfortunately, many places are not sensory friendly simply by nature. Even more unfortunate are the judgmental and uneducated people out there who give the dirty looks and glares when a child is melting down or just simply can't sit still on the airplane. This all makes me so, so sad.

But we must move forward and conquer and educate and spread SPD awareness! And the best part is our society is indeed starting to understand SPD and even the term "sensory" is being used more often and taken with acceptance and compassion rather than the "huh?" look on the person's face.

Through spreading awareness and understanding our sensory kiddos' needs in EVERY situation . . . including the hotel, or the amusement park…we can improve their quality of life AND make for a pleasant trip or vacation for the whole darn family. ☺

2 ROAD TRIP

The oh so dreaded road trip….

Hours of packing and preparing and loading the SUV with all of the snacks, coloring books, DVDs, and favorite pillows and blankies and it is time to hit the road! Only to encounter your first meltdown 30 minutes after jumping on the freeway.

You tell yourself…why did we do this? I knew this would happen! This is going to be miserable (and a few other choice words). How will we possibly get through the next 3 days? Let's just turn around and go home.

But being the determined parent that you are, you keep on driving. Climbing over the front seat, bottom stuck to the roof of the car to try to reach the favorite stuffed animal that just got chucked during a moment of meltdown to then hopefully console and quiet the child. You sit back down in the passengers seat and take a deep breath. "We can do this," you say in your head. Only to then hear the screech and scream of "She hit me!!!!!". You turn back again and give a warning, "No hitting or we will turn around and go home!" You then offer more snacks or suggest a fun, keep- them-busy toy.

The screaming continues, the lashing out continues…and then comes the barf. (Sorry for the gross language, but it just seems so appropriate) No warning, just a huge disgusting mess all over the clothes, the car seat, and the floor. Hopefully at least the sibling was spared.

You pull the SUV over to clean up the stinky mess, change the child's clothes, and console him. Everyone decides to get out for a stretch break and a potty break…then a few more deep breaths, and you hit the road again.

There are so many sensory factors and variables involved in a road trip. Of course every sensory kiddo has their unique sensory needs and differences, but I will discuss some of the most common sensory issues and then most importantly some suggestions on how to make the road trip a little more pleasant. ☺

Let's start with…

STRATEGIC POSITIONING IN THE VEHICLE

Depending on how many siblings are involved, and the age of the sensory kiddos as well as the sensory needs and differences, the placement of the child can be crucial. Is the child sensitive to sound or touch? If so, and if possible, have the child positioned in the back and alone. If they are positioned right behind the front seats, then they get a whole lot of auditory input from siblings or others in the vehicle. Like sitting in the movie theater…if you are in the back you do not get all of the auditory distractions of those chomping popcorn or talking.

And it may seem cruel or isolating to not have the child sit next to anyone, but believe me, they will thank you in the long run. It will decrease the urge to touch or lash out at others, and on the opposite side of the coin, will decrease the chances of the child being touched or brushed against, which could cause a meltdown if tactile issues are present.

One last suggestion…if a parent can sit next to the child or an older sibling…one who understands the child's sensory needs and is a good sensory match for them . . . this would be a wise choice as well. Having a healthy sensory buddy next to you for deep pressure arm and hand rubs or being available to quietly interact with can be a wonderful thing.

LOTS AND LOTS OF SENSORY BREAKS

I realize this may sound like a real hassle, but wouldn't it be better to be taking healthy sensory breaks rather than the REQUIRED negative road trip breaks?

I would suggest at least stopping once an hour…and not just for a potty break…I mean a real sensory break! Run, climb a tree, stop at a park, have wheelbarrow races at the rest area, move move move!

These ever so needed sensory breaks help everyone's brain regulate and especially for the sensory kiddo. Movement breaks and added heavy/hard work (proprioception) breaks will help the child cope and maintain a ready state for continuation of the road trip.

ORAL SENSORY NEEDS AND TREATS

Even if the child is not necessarily an oral seeker, meeting oral sensory needs while on a road trip are crucial for self-regulation. Of course if the child is a sensory seeker, then be sure you have their oral sensory tool/chewy with you and definitely a back up or two! It is inevitable that on a trip the chewy gets lost! The best types of snacks for sensory kids are chewy or crunchy. Gum is great as well for children old enough to chew it. Stop for a milkshake or smoothie along the way too…the resistive sucking is excellent for self-regulation. A CamelBak® water bottle is my favorite for use with water in the car, as it has a great mouthpiece for chewing on and requires resistive sucking. Some kids like an oral sensory tool that vibrates, as it can be calming and soothing. You can even bring along a vibrating toothbrush!

THE RIGHT TYPE OF SENSORY TOYS

Be sure you bring along your child's favorite fidget toys, more than one is best, with various textures and various squeeze options…your child's sensory mood will change throughout the trip. Theraband® is an excellent tool to use in the car, and you can tie a piece to the door handle and your child can pull on it for the resistance and proprioception. Other great road trip sensory toys include Silly Putty®, Magna Doodle®, Lauri Toys Toddler Tote®, Lauri Toys Primer Pack®, Alex Toys My First Mosiac®, Melissa & Doug License Plate game®, and Wikki Stix®.

SENSORY TOOLS

Depending on your child, there will be a few essential sensory tools that will make for a much more enjoyable trip. These tools may include earplugs or noise cancelling headphones, an MP3 player with the child's favorite soothing music, a weighted lap pad or blanket, a compression vest, sunglasses, wide brimmed hat, vibrating pillow, and of course the oral sensory tools already mentioned.

MEALS

I know it is so tempting to just whip through the drive thru somewhere and get the adored chicken nuggets…but if possible, only do this in moderation on the trip. Pack as much food as you can with healthier options full of protein and not full of preservatives, additives, and dyes. Pack crunchy carrot sticks and apples as an alternative, or turkey jerky is awesome, too. Often the food your child eats on a trip can be the culprit to the sensory dysregulation and meltdowns. The best sensory options I would suggest are the drive thrus where you can get a smoothie or a milkshake!

BATHROOM BREAKS AND BATHROOM URGENCY

Sensory kiddos often have a difficult time registering the need to go to the bathroom until the very last minute. This is due to the interoceptors in the gut (like proprioceptors) having a difficult time giving sensory feedback to the brain in regards to "it's time to go potty". It is important to respect this with sensory children, and know that if they suddenly say….I GOTTA GO POTTY! …they mean it. During those ever so frequent sensory breaks you are going to take, use those also as an opportunity to go to the bathroom. But please be tolerant and understanding if your trip requires yet another potty stop.

THE EVER SO DREADED… "I AM GONNA THROW UP"

I saved the best for last. ☺ Car sickness is very much linked to sensory processing difficulties, especially if the child has difficulty with processing vestibular input (movement). Being in a car becomes extra difficult for a sensory kiddo when there a lot of starts and stops, as well as a curvy road. Usually a sensory child is not able to read, or attend visually to something due to this vestibular issue. A few tips that may help include:

- Cover the window the child is sitting next to with a pillow case (this cuts down the peripheral visual input which can trigger car sickness).
- Position the child in the car so he can see directly out the front window (middle seat).
- Avoid any riding sideways or backwards, such as some seats in trucks and SUVs.
- Providing an oral sensory tool or Camelbak® water bottle to suck on with water or a sour beverage.
- Lemon drops are known to help nausea.

- Travel at night when the child is sleeping, so the eyes are closed and the visual component is not a trigger.
- Using other sensory tools which the child typically responds well to can also be helpful.
- Don't forget the barf bag or bucket….sensory kiddos often are unable to give you warning when it is time to throw up.

3 AIRPLANES

I must first begin by saying I wish there were more understanding, empathetic, and compassionate people in this world. It is one thing to have a not so nice person living down the street, or passing someone in the grocery store who gives you a glare when your child is having a sensory meltdown…but an AIRPLANE?! Could there be a worse place for Mrs. Grumpy Pants?!

The close quarters and "tight spaces" may be wonderful for sensory kiddos at home…but the airplane is the last "tight space" a sensory child wants to be in. There are sooooooooooo many factors which make air travel difficult.

- Lack of vestibular and proprioceptive input, and the inability to get it when they need it.
- Unfamiliar and unpredictable auditory input. The airplane bathroom toilet flushing sound is enough to send anyone into sensory overload.
- Unpleasant sensations such as ears popping, and possible internal

discomfort when the plane is taking off and landing due to vestibular intolerance.

- LONG periods of time required to be seated.
- So many restrictions and rules to follow.
- Typically parents are a little stressed and not in the most relaxed state of mind to help the sensory kiddo. (Probably because of the possible Mrs. Grumpy Pants on board.)
- The airplane seats are very hard and uncomfortable, not conducive to the soft, nest like feel a sensory child needs.
- The option for play and activities are pretty darn limited.
- Did I mention Mrs. Grumpy Pants? ☺

LET'S MAKE THE MOST OUT OF IT

Since air travel is sometimes just necessary, all we can do is cope, adapt, tolerate, and be prepared with sensory tools and strategies!

Many of the recommendations I made in the ROAD TRIP chapter also apply on the airplane…but I will list them here again for ease of reading.

IN THE AIRPORT & A PORTABLE SENSORY RETREAT

If your child is a sensory seeker, now is the time to let your child run, hop, skip, jump, etc! They need it to help self-regulate when they are on the plane. Please do not discourage it! Also, bring along a stroller even for a little bit older kids…a jogging stroller is ideal, for a portable sensory retreat. A jogging stroller is the best because it wraps around the child's body and provide deep pressure touch. It also typically has a canopy over it, in which you can then drape a blanket over that to create a cozy tent feeling in the stroller. This is your portable sensory retreat ☺. You can then add a weighted blanket, weighted lap pad, oral sensory tools, fidget toy, and other appropriate sensory tools. Believe me, you will not only be using this portable sensory retreat in the airport, but it will also come in handy along the trip many times. ☺

STRATEGIC POSITIONING ON THE AIRPLANE

Depending on how many siblings are involved, and the age of the sensory kiddos as well as the sensory needs and differences, the placement of the sensory child can be crucial. Is the child sensitive to touch? If so, and if possible, have the child positioned at the window seat. Sitting in the center or on the aisle are much more difficult for those not liking to be touched or brushed against. Be sure the most appropriate family member is sitting next to them, even if they request otherwise! If a parent can sit next to the child or an older sibling…one who understands the child's sensory needs and is a good sensory match for them, this would be a best. Having a healthy sensory buddy next to you for deep pressure arm and hand rubs or being available to quietly interact with can be a wonderful thing.

If possible, request at check in or when you make the reservation to be seated in the front. (I know this is opposite of what I suggested for a road trip, but I will explain). The closer you are to the front…the very front seats would be ideal…the less effect the possible crying/screaming/loud sounds your child may make will have on others. This is very stressful for parents and such a big worry on the plane. You can request this at check in and be sure to mention that you have a child with special needs and accommodations due to sensory processing disorder. The airline staff will likely do their best to accommodate. Don't be afraid to explain the scenario a little bit to them and let them know how making the accommodations can help everyone!

TRYING TO CREATE A SENSORY BREAK

As we know, this is extremely limited, but here are a few suggestions that can help.

- Prior to boarding the plane be sure to have the kiddo get a powerful dose of vestibular and proprioceptive input…5-10 minutes will do. Let the child run in the airport or march, hop, jump, etc. If there are stairs around…let them climb them a few times. Hang your child upside down for a minute. (Inverting the head is excellent vestibular input!) Wheelbarrow walk the child around a little. Who cares if people look at you weird! You are advocating and doing what is best for your child's sensory needs!

- Also be sure to make time for a sensory break during a layover during the trip! Refrain from asking your child to sit and wait at the gate…let them move, move move! Yes, it takes some effort to supervise, but you will thank me later.
- When it is safe to do so during flight, let your child pace the aisle for a little while…it can at least get the wiggles out a tiny bit. And once again, don't worry about what Mrs. Grumpy Pants is thinking. ☺
- While in the seat (and it is safe to unbuckle) have your child squat in the seat, do chair push ups, even let them stand for a minute if they are small enough. I would even recommend letting them do a headstand in the seat (it really would be good for them!) but I bet this would send the flight attendant through the roof of the plane. ☺

ORAL SENSORY NEEDS AND TREATS

Even if the child is not necessarily an oral seeker, meeting oral sensory needs while on the airplane is crucial for self-regulation. Of course, if the child is a sensory seeker, then be sure you have their oral sensory tool/chewy with you and definitely a back up or two! It is inevitable that on a trip the chewy gets lost! The best types of snacks for sensory kids are chewy or crunchy. Gum is great as well for children old enough to chew it…and is also excellent for helping those painful popping ears. Purchase a milkshake or smoothie prior to boarding or during a layover…the resistive sucking is excellent for self-regulation. A CamelBak® water bottle is my favorite for use with water on the plane as well, it has a great mouthpiece for chewing on and it requires resistive sucking. Just watch out! The pressure in the plane can make the water squirt out a little…and possibly alarming for your little one. Some kids like an oral sensory tool that vibrates, and it can be calming and soothing. You can even bring along a vibrating toothbrush!

THE RIGHT TYPE OF SENSORY TOYS

Be sure you bring along your child's favorite fidget toys, more than one is best, with various textures and various squeeze options…your child's sensory mood will change throughout the trip. Theraband® is an excellent tool to use on the airplane, and you can tie a piece to the arm rest and your child can pull on it for the resistance and proprioception Other great airplane sensory toys include Silly Putty®, Magna Doodle®, Lauri Toys Toddler Tote®, Lauri Toys Primer Pack®, Alex Toys My First Mosiac®, and Wikki Stix®. A portable DVD player is not a bad idea at all in this scenario either, especially if your child "gets in the zone" with a favorite movie.

SENSORY TOOLS

Depending on your child, there will be a few essential sensory tools that will make for a much more tolerable plane ride. These tools may include earplugs or noise cancelling headphones, an MP3 player with the child's favorite soothing music, a weighted lap pad or blanket, a compression vest, sunglasses, wide brimmed hat, vibrating pillow, and of course the oral sensory tools already mentioned. The auditory tools may also be needed for sensory kiddos who typically wouldn't need them…there is such a large amount of unpredictable auditory input on an airplane. The sunglasses and hat may be necessary to help create somewhat of a "faux sensory retreat" due to all of the social demands involved with being on a plane. Let the child cope a little better with all of the sensations and the strange surroundings by keeping to themselves under the big hat and sunglasses…its ok…its not the time to work on social skills…I promise you that one.

THE SPECIAL GADGETS ON AN AIRPLANE

The airplane is full of fun little buttons, levers, and such which you only see on an airplane. It's OKAY if your child wants to open and close and open and close the window shade and the tray! It really is. Please refrain from choosing this battle ☺. The person in front of them would have a lot more to contend with if you insisted on not touching the fun little levers and such.

The buttons above you…go ahead and let your child explore them once instead of saying they are off limits…let him get it out of his system. Keep in mind the air knob may cause a reaction for some kiddos if they struggle with tactile defensiveness, the air blowing on their little face may be painful. Please also keep this in mind when they are seated…the air may be a sensory trigger for problems.

In the bathroom…all sorts of fun things to explore in there! Again…let them explore the faucet and the paper towels and tissues…not the toilet though! Back away from the toilet! (If indeed that were really possible in there) But seriously, this may sound horrible and wrong…but after your child goes to the bathroom, do NOT flush it. Return to your seat and if you feel so inclined to return and flush it without your child with you, then go for it. Even with your child standing right outside the door, it can be so loud and trigger sensory overload.

THE DREADED AIRPLANE MELTDOWN

I saved the best for last. (Just like in the last chapter) ☺
Just be prepared and expect at least one meltdown or at least a little sensory dysregulation out of your child. It will likely happen, so if you are prepared and expecting it…it can go a little smoother.

Hopefully with the advice and suggestions I have given, your sensory kiddo will have the sensory tools and strategies to help get through the trip. But there is always the unexpected "bumps in the road/air" (literally) that are unpredictable and simply out of our control. If this does happen here are my suggestions:

- Remain calm. Your child will feed off of your stress and response to the situation. Be the solid and regulated rock that they need at that moment.
- Provide deep pressure touch or a bear hug and sit quietly with the child. Do not try to quiet her with words or rationalize with her...it will only make the situation worse and last longer.

- Offer an oral sensory tool…this is a very good way to help soothe and calm the child.
- If there is a sensory trigger which can be removed or addressed at the moment, assess the situation and respond accordingly.
- Create a makeshift sensory retreat using a blanket or weighted blanket if you brought one…cover the child entirely with the blanket and provide gentle pressure to the body. Hopefully they will have tried to curl up in flexion. (Like fetal position.) Flexion is the most organizing type of input.
- Use noise cancelling headphones if you have them.

NOT THE TIME TO WORK ON SOCIAL GRACES

Please try to refrain from showing the world that you are a great parent and that you have taught your child manners. This is not the time for your child to initiate or engage in a conversation with the flight attendant or the guy at security, nor is it the time to request even a simple please or thank you. Just let your child be quiet, bury his/her head in your chest, or hide under a blanket or hat to avoid eye contact. It's ok, it really is. All that really matters during this time is that your sensory kiddo stays as regulated as possible and avoids sensory overload. Insisting on manners and social interaction can create dysregulation and sensory overload in a time like this.

4 STAYING WITH RELATIVES OR FRIENDS

Most of us personally have a story or have heard a story about the uncle, mother-in-law, or a friend who thinks they have all of the answers to parenting ☺. Now bring in the sensory factor and you just created your worst nightmare.

Educating those around us about SPD and sensory differences is the very best strategy in advocating for our sensory kiddos. And this is an absolutely crucial link when you are visiting and/or staying with friends or relatives.

My first suggestion is prior to the visit, begin your SPD awareness campaign with your hosts! You choose the best avenue based on the individual...it may be a phone call and discussion about SPD and the possible situations that may arise during the visit. It may be mailing a sensory handbook to them, such as *Understanding Your Child's Sensory Signals*, which is easy to read and makes sense to one not so familiar with SPD. If you send them something too wordy and complicated it won't get read, simple as that. Maybe simply an email or letter explaining the upcoming visits and some of the modifications that may need to be made would be effective.

Now if you do not feel the friends or relatives are going to be receptive to this...then stay somewhere else. It is going to be difficult for your sensory kiddo staying away from home as it is, and you do NOT need the added stress of someone possibly not respecting your child's sensory differences and needs.

ASSESSING YOUR SURROUNDINGS

Upon arrival to your new temporary landing pad, it will be important to determine if there are any specific sensory triggers which may be a challenge . . . such as a jumping, barking dog. Adapt as needed. Encourage the use of noise cancelling headphones and talk with your kiddo about a possible plan to limit the unexpected jumps from the dog.

Look for your prime sensory tools as well…maybe a trampoline in the backyard or a therapy ball in the house. You will want to show your child where the appropriate places will be to get their crucial sensory input. If it is not really a kid-friendly house, then it will be necessary to come up with a game plan with the host. Based on your child's sensory needs…discuss this with the host and come up with a plan.

SLEEPING ARRANGEMENTS

This is probably the most challenging part for sensory kiddos, yet the most important to address. If your child uses a weighted blanket, be sure to bring it along on the trip. If you use music or white noise, bring this as well. Since staying in an unfamiliar house is difficult for all of us, be sure to make a special cozy little sensory retreat for your child to sleep in. (The retreat will be multi-purpose) Create a cozy corner with lots of pillows and blankets, or make a squish box with supplies in the home. If you are lucky enough, and your host has a twin size duvet cover, make a pillow cave as well!

For the pillow cave: using the twin size duvet…fill it up with blankets, pillows, and stuffed animals…let the child go inside as a sensory retreat, and at bedtime, fluff it up in the corner of a room and have your child sleep on it like a nest. Of course this is only recommended for children who are mobile and able to maneuver their body in the nest safely.

For the squish box: use a large plastic tote or laundry basket….just the right size of a container for your child to sit in and get squished a little. Add a couple blankets and pillows to make it cozy. This provides full body deep pressure touch and proprioception to help the child's nervous system regulate.

Another option for a weighted blanket is to use a heavy quilt or denim blanket folded into a large square, just the right size to drape over your child. Folding it creates a more dense, heavy blanket.

Make sure you have brought along your child's favorite blanket, oral sensory tool, cuddle toy, and any other important sensory tool that helps your child sleep.

And last but not least, be sure to provide full body deep pressure touch/squeezes at bedtime. This will help your child's nervous system transition to sleep easier in an unfamiliar place.

MEALTIME

Sensory kiddos often struggle with food issues already…and then you add in the "have to sit still" factor and the social interaction with those at the table. This is likely going to be much more challenging during your visit. The child may not be comfortable with the people at the table, it may be louder than usual, and the food may be different than what is typically served at home. All of these components can create a real sensory challenge for your child! Please be sensitive to this and respectful of the fact that it may be incredibly difficult to face all of these different components of mealtime.

Here are my suggestions…

- Prior to the group situation, prepare the child's nervous system with a 15-minute movement and heavy/hard work activity.
- Keep in mind that 10-15 minutes at the dinner table will likely be the maximum amount of time the child can handle. A kid friendly side table with a ball chair as the seat would be best, or just the kid friendly table.

- Asking the child to try new foods during an already challenging sensory experience may be out of the question. The child's nervous system is already stressed. Provide safe and comforting healthy foods which the child likes. I know, you may get some "feedback" on this one…this is one of the topics you can discuss prior to the visit. ☺

SOCIALIZING AND PLAYTIME

Socializing and interacting with unfamiliar adults and playing with unfamiliar children will indeed be a huge challenge for your sensory kiddo. There can be so many factors and variables…

- The pitch, frequency, speed of speech, and volume of sound of those around the child. It may be overwhelming to the child. Be sure to be sensitive to this and modify as needed. The child may need more frequent sensory retreat breaks or possibly earplugs or noise cancelling headphones. Keep in mind this may be a factor during the trip, even though auditory input may not typically effect the child.

- The amount of touch and type of touch given by those around them. Constant hugs, love pats, or kisses may be just too much for them. These are usually coming in at a greater rate than on a typical day.
- The type of interaction during play. Is the other child "in your face" or very active and overwhelming in play? Do they like to constantly wrestle?
- On the other hand…maybe your child is the one being the "in your face and space" and constantly wanting to wrestle. Make sure the other child involved is a good match for this.
- Do not insist on eye contact, hugs/kisses, or even verbal communication while your child is being introduced or interacting with new and unfamiliar people. This is incredibly difficult for sensory kiddos. More information on this topic is found in *Understanding Your Child's Sensory Signals.*

A SENSORY RETREAT

A sensory retreat will be a crucial component during your stay with relatives or friends. Your sensory child may need this retreat on a regular basis during your stay and should indeed be the safe place to retreat to during sensory overload, fight or flight, or just when needing a place to re-group, re-set, and get a nice dose of proprioception.

You can create a sensory retreat with household items. Be creative! You can also use the jogging stroller which was discussed in the AIRPLANE chapter for those children small enough to use it. Here are a few other ideas…

- A squish box in a nice quiet and dim room. Make the squish box with a laundry basket or plastic tote, add blankets and pillows and have your child "squish into it". Add their favorite fidget toy, an oral sensory tool, or a weighted item as well.
- A pillow cave, which you may be using for sleep as well. You may need to bring the twin size duvet cover from home…but then add pillows and blankets and soft items from the host's

home. Have the child go inside the pillow cave, or fluff it up in the corner of a room and have the child get cozy on it like a nest. Add the same items as listed for the squish box.

- Drape a blanket over a small table and place this in a quiet room. Add cozy and comfortable items underneath the table, including other sensory tools.
- A cozy quiet spot in a walk-in closet can work as well.

KEEPING SOMEWHAT OF A ROUTINE

I realize this is easier said than done. But please, please, please try your best to keep somewhat of a routine! Our sensory kiddos THRIVE on it! And it can make all of the difference in self-regulation and the child's ability to cope with all of the new sensory input and new environment during the stay!

SENSORY TOOLS

I have already mentioned quite a few sensory tools to be utilized during your stay with relatives or friends. And since you have likely travelled to this location via plane or car…then you already have your sensory tools with you! Whooo hoooo!

5 HOTELS

WHAT TO LOOK FOR IN A HOTEL

Here are a few starting suggestions when you are choosing your hotel. Even though it may cost a little more, it will likely make your stay a whole lot more pleasant. And nothing is more helpful than a good night's sleep for your sensory kiddo and the rest of the family.

- Stay away from rooms with a wall unit for heat and air conditioning. I know these are very common, but many hotels have a central heating and air conditioning system. This can be so helpful since the constant auditory input of it turning on/off can keep a sensory child up all night.
- Be sure the hotel has a pool…this may indeed be your sensory saving grace during the hotel stay.
- Some outdoor space for running around would be ideal. Or at least a kid friendly hotel where the child can run up and down the halls a little.

YOUR CHECK-IN REQUESTS

It is important to be pro-active and prepare as much as possible for staying at a hotel. This preparation begins when you book your room reservation. If you wait until check-in for special requests, the hotel may not be able to honor them based on availability, so be sure to address then when you book your room! Here are my suggestions for special requests….

- Request a quiet room away from the elevator, any freeway noise, or any common areas. Sensory kiddos often hear everything.
- Request a rollaway bed and a bunch of extra pillows and even an extra comforter (not just the cheap flimsy blankets) that you can push up into the corner of the room and create a cozy nest for some extra proprioception. Do not be afraid to ask for as many as you think your child may need!
- If your child is small enough, bring along a pack and play and create a nice cozy nest in there for your child to sleep in.

SLEEPING ARRANGEMENTS

Based on the those suggestions, create the most conducive place for your sensory child to sleep. Sleeping with a sibling might not be the best idea. Paying a little extra money for the rollaway will very likely be worth it. Also be sure to bring along a weighted blanket if you have one, your child's most comfortable jammies, and also a white noise machine or a music player with the normal bedtime music. The key is to keep as many things as consistent with home as possible. Sensory kiddos thrive on consistency and routine! It will be well worth it to haul along the extra items and take the extra steps. The alternative may be a grumpy and dysregulated child.

Try very hard to stay on the normal home sleep schedule during your entire trip.

THE POOL

Swimming is an excellent tool for much needed proprioception. Proprioceptive input is regulating, organizing, and calming. You will most likely want to use the pool as a sensory tool during your stay. You do want to choose quiet times at the pool so the sensory tool doesn't backfire on you. Often right when the pool opens in the morning around 10am is a great time, and this is also an effective way to prep your child's nervous system for the day. Don't forget to bring the goggles from home!

SENSORY BREAKS

Now I know if any hotel owners or companies get a hold of this book they are going to go through the roof…but a little bit of supervised jumping on the beds is excellent for the nervous system ☺.

Hopefully the hotel has an outdoor play area, but if not, then maybe some wheelbarrow or crab walking in the hallways, and some running up and down the stairs will do the brain some good. You have to get creative with your sensory breaks and activities in the hotel. Sometimes the workout rooms have large exercise balls…if so, you can request to borrow one to use with your child. If you explain your situation, the hotel staff will likely be accommodating.

6 THE BEACH

The beach can be a wonderful, peaceful, memorable experience of a lifetime for a child…but this can be a whole different story for a sensory kiddo. It may seem very peaceful and relaxing, but there are SO many sensory factors that come into play. As a parent, it is important to see this experience through your "sensory goggles" and determine which sensory triggers may be an issue for your child.

THE SAND

Now if you have a sensory seeker at heart who loves tactile experiences, than you have it made! Your little sensory seeker is going to dig, bury, roll, run, and jump in the sand. And it can also be an excellent proprioceptive and heavy/hard work activity while they are playing in the sand, which will help regulate and calm the nervous system. On the other hand…sometimes a child who typically enjoys different textures may indeed have difficulty with the sand because of the overwhelming amount of sensory input involved and the amount of sand on the beach. Quite different than just a sandbox.☺ So it is important to be prepared for whatever sensory twist may come your way. Here are some helpful tips….

- Do NOT just plop your child down into the sand in bare feet and a swimming suit or swimming trunks! Begin by sitting the child in a low to the ground beach chair, and let the child lead the way. If and when they are ready to explore the texture, they will. Do NOT force it.
- If your child is extremely tactilely defensive, I would recommend nice snug neoprene water shoes which cover the feet and give deep pressure.
- Provide plenty of sand tools so the child can first explore the sand that way.
- Wet sand and dry sand have completely different textures…offer the opportunity for both. Your child may tolerate one better than the other.
- I would also suggest a rash guard shirt for girls and boys to cover their chest/trunk if they are defensive to the sand. Rash guards also serve as a compression garment which will provide regulating proprioception during your time at the beach. A snug fitting life jacket is not only a great tool for safety, but it also provides deep pressure/compression as well!

- Having your child wear goggles while playing in the sand is not a bad idea either, since even a tiny bit of sand near or in the eye can send a sensory kiddo into fight or flight.

THE WIND

Wind is often a factor at the beach…especially on the Pacific ocean in the northwest! Wind can be especially noxious and uncomfortable for sensory children…because it is unpredictable, comes in different strengths, and in this case, can blow the sand. OUCH! One little grain of sand blown at a sensory kiddo's face can be extremely painful and scary. Here are my suggestions…

- Avoid the beach on a super windy day…it just simply isn't worth it. Breezy is ok, but real windy will likely be just way too much if your child is a sensory avoider.
- The sensory tools I recommend are a rash guard and a sweatshirt or wind breaker with a hood, if it is one of the cooler days. Earplugs or noise cancelling headphones can be helpful, as well as sunglasses or goggles and a big floppy hat with a chin strap, of course. ☺

THE SUN

The sun can be very draining for all of us at the beach, and you guessed it, even more draining for a sensory kiddo. The sun may also be way too bright for your child, so it is important to be prepared for this. Here are some ideas to help…

- Polarized sunglasses
- Big floppy hat
- Portable umbrella for shade
- Sun screen, of course
- Rash guard
- Tons of drinking water…not sweetened drinks or juice, and definitely not soda pop

THE WATER

The ocean is obviously quite different than the pool. So keep in mind your little sensory swimmer may not be as fond of the ocean. All it takes is for one little thing to be different…and the idea of swimming is out of the question for a sensory kiddo. The ocean is in constant motion with waves in all different size, the water looks different, smells different, and tastes different. There are two scenarios which I want to bring up….

If you have an extreme sensory seeker you MUST be so cautious and careful with a watchful eye. A sensory seeker can get in a "sensory tunnel" and if the ocean looks just way too inviting, then all safety and judgment blows away in the breeze. Even if you call for the child to stop or come back, they truly may not process it and "hear" you.

On the other hand, a sensory avoider may be downright scared and overwhelmed. Do not force the issue…it will be a huge accomplishment for the child to simply put his feet in the water and experience the waves. If the child does want to wade a little more and lay in the wet sand near the edge of the waves, goggles and swimmers earplugs are strongly recommended.

BEST BEACH ACTIVITIES FOR A SENSORY KIDDO

After now completing this chapter, you see that the beach can be a challenging place for a sensory child. But it can be a successful and pleasant experience with the right sensory knowledge and tools.

Every sensory kiddo is different and it will take wearing your "sensory goggles" to determine which sensory experiences the child is avoiding and seeking out at the beach. But involving proprioception is a great idea no matter what. So running on the beach, digging in the sand, walking through the deep sand, and frolicking in the waves and doing a little swimming are all excellent proprioceptive activities. ☺

A PORTABLE SENSORY RETREAT ON THE BEACH

For a child who is small enough…probably through the toddler ages…you can bring along a Pack N Play® type playpen to set up on the beach and fill it with some soft pillows and a blanket, and then cover the whole thing with a lightweight sheet. This can serve as a nice sensory retreat. If you brought the jogging stroller on the trip, this can also be a good portable retreat as discussed in previous chapters.

7 CAMPING AND HIKING

THE CAMPSITE

Camping provides so many wonderful opportunities for sensory exploration, especially tactile input. For the sensory seekers, it will be important to determine exploration boundaries, and even then a close watchful eye will be needed since the child may get in that "sensory tunnel" and keep on exploring. For the sensory avoiders…bring along some child-size gardening gloves so they can enjoy exploring as well. Also bringing along a bucket for gathering "treasures" provides a heavy work activity, and it also decreases frustration for the child who is trying to gather in their little hands every stick, pinecone, and stone they find. Sensory kiddos tend to be real gatherers of treasures. ☺

The campfire will be very tempting for the sensory seeker. So my suggestion is to incorporate a heavy/hard work activity to help create a safe boundary for them. Usually a fire pit has some sort of boundary, but I suggest creating a ring with decent size rocks around the parameter of the fire pit, at a greater distance than normal. Your child will love being in charge of this fun and regulating task!

TOOLS FOR SLEEPING

Sleeping in a tent or camper is difficult for many of us, and will likely be extra difficult for your sensory child. Earplugs or noise cancelling headphones is the first thing that comes to my mind. The night time sounds are one of the most unique sensory components of camping….and often sensory kiddos hear EVERYTHING. As discussed in previous chapter about sleep…you will want to bring along as many of your child's normal sensory tools for sleep. And if sleeping in a tent, be extra diligent in providing a nice soft, cozy surface for your child to sleep on. The sleeping bag will also likely be your child's best friend. It may even be their little sensory retreat during the camping trip. ☺

EXPLORE, EXPLORE, EXPLORE

Take this opportunity to let your sensory seeker go for it! What a beautiful time and place to let your child dig in the dirt, touch all of the different textures of plants and trees, discover new little bugs and critters, run/climb/skip/hop and simply explore their sensory world! Try your very best to be mindful of this and put as few restrictions in place as possible…of course safety and respect for nature comes first, but then let them EXPLORE!!!!

HIKING

Hiking is an absolutely awesome activity for self-regulation! Hiking involves a HUGE amount of proprioception. Encourage your child to climb hills and rocks, jump off of rocks and logs. This is also great for body awareness, balance, and overall gross motor development. Also encourage your child to walk along logs!

I would suggest hiking at times during your camping trip when you feel your child may need a dose of self-regulating and calming input. Yet I would caution you . . . it is important to gauge and monitor the distance of the hike…or you may be "backpacking" your kiddo back to the campsite. It is very common for a sensory kiddo to be "hot or cold"…when they are done, they are done. Period.

Speaking of backpacks…for the little ones, hiking can still be a wonderful sensory experience while being carried in the infant/toddler packs. The child will experience a great amount of full body deep pressure touch and also vestibular input during the hike. But be sure to let the little one out for moments of hiking and sensory exploration as well. ☺

It is very important to bring a ton of water while hiking and my favorite tool in this case is the Camelbak® water bottle, which comes in all sizes! There are also Camelbak® water backpacks which have an excellent mouthpiece for an oral sensory tool and the backpack comes in adult and child sizes.

8 AMUSEMENT PARKS

Let me first begin by mentioning that if it is at all possible, schedule your trip to an amusement park on the OFF SEASON. This can make such a difference in the overall experience.

YOUR CLASSIC MULTI-SENSORY ENVIRONMENT

Multi-sensory experiences, even the grocery store, can be overwhelming and very difficult for a sensory kiddo. Now an amusement park takes it to a whole new level. ☺

Let's begin with visual input….so much to take in from all of the colorful rides and displays, possibly large dressed up characters, and all of the people walking around. So much to see and take in from the visual side of things…AND the sunlight as well.

Next would be auditory input…this can be a REAL challenge. Music, unexpected and unpredictable buzzing and beeping sounds, children screaming and squealing in delight, people talking, loud announcements on the rides, etc.

Tactile input…this can simply be difficult from walking from one ride to the next. People brushing and bumping against you, constantly in your "personal bubble".

Vestibular input…lots of walking and possibly riding in a stroller or wagon or in a backpack just scratches the surface of all of the possible movement experiences which may be in store throughout the day. Where else are you going to experience movement in all possible body positions and in every plane and direction of movement, at all different speeds?

THE RIDES

It is important to remember that each and every ride is not just the actual ride itself. It is also a combination of sensory input typically involving all of the senses mentioned above, along with the component of the unknown, unpredictability, anticipation, and the possibility of sensory overload and the inability to tolerate the new vestibular experience.

If your child is a sensory seeker, then this may be a little easier, except for the fact that even a sensory seeker can develop sensory overload in a new multi-sensory experience like this. Vestibular input is extremely powerful and this must be respected and taken into consideration for all children at an amusement park. Watch for signs of sensory overload including systemic reactions such as flushing of the face, nausea, fever, etc.

For a sensory avoider or a child who has difficulty with tolerating movement, an amusement park is NOT the place to work on tolerating movement. Be prepared for this, and trying to talk the child into it or bribing them is actually very unfair to your sensory kiddo. Simply respect the fact that if they say no, they mean no.

For all sensory children, spending time on the nice calming rides can be very beneficial, such as the monorail or train. This can provide a necessary dose of calming and regulating input and help the brain sort out all of the intense sensory input the child has been trying to process.

Also, be sure to utilize the play areas where your child can get a good dose of proprioception from climbing, hanging, jumping, etc. Many of the big theme parks have huge climbing structures and play zones for children.

STANDING IN LINE

Hanging on the bars while waiting in line really is ok…matter of fact it is good for them ☺. Hanging provides joint traction to the arms (proprioception), which is regulating, calming, and organizing. And we all know standing in line at an amusement park is not an easy task for any of us!

Just imagine how it may feel for a little sensory seeker. This is also a great time to hold your child and let him play some monkey games by hanging from your arms or hanging upside down while you hold the feet. Also try the panda bear game with your child latched onto your leg and see how long they can hang on. Change his perspective…have the child sit on your shoulders or give him a piggy back ride! This is also a good time to pull out some of your sensory tools in your travel bag…such as a fidget toy, music with headphones, oral sensory tool, and the Camelbak® water bottle, or even a crunchy or chewy snack.

Now for the sensory avoider, standing in line is downright difficult. The close proximity of the people brushing against the child by accident, in addition to the auditory and visual input, can be overwhelming. Do not be surprised if your child wants to simply be held and bury her face against your body. This is a good time to use noise cancelling headphones or an MP3 player with soft calming music. A big floppy hat and sunglasses may also be helpful if the child is overwhelmed by all of the visual input and potential eye contact from others.

The good part about all of this, is that many amusement/theme parks now offer a fast track pass or guest assistance card or other options and modifications for those with special needs. This includes SPD of course. But often there is even a long wait in the alternate line…so it may be helpful to use some of these ideas listed above.

Another thing to keep in mind and respect for your child is that they may wait in line and say they want to go on the ride, but it may be a whole different story when it is your turn. You may need to stand there and let others in front of you, over and over again, as the transition from standing in line to the anticipation of getting on a ride with unknown and unpredictable sensory input may be completely overwhelming. Try to be patient. Take deep breaths…both of you. And even let the rest of the family go ahead while one parent or adult waits with the child until ready. Keep in mind that they might not get to the point of being ready, and you may need to walk away. Respect this and accept it…if you get frustrated this will only lead to further difficulty with self-regulation for your sensory kiddo.

DO NOT INSIST ON SOCIAL INTERACTION

Do not ask your child to make eye contact or talk to the staff or others around them. This is an extremely difficult time for them and is not the time to work on social interaction.

THE PORTABLE SENSORY RETREAT

The good ol' jogging stroller, wagon, or other type of stroller which I talked about in previous chapters will likely be your best friend on your amusement park adventure. It will be your sensory kiddo's safe place and mini/portable sensory retreat.

The main components of the portable sensory retreat need to be:

- Cozy and squishy (lots of blankets and a stuffed animal or pillow)
- Use a blanket to cover the entire stroller to minimize all sensory input.
- Something weighted if possible, such as a weighted lap pad or blanket
- Fidget toy and possibly a vibrating toy or vibrating pillow
- Oral sensory tools
- Crunchy and chewy snacks
- Earplugs or noise cancelling headphones, MP3 player with soft and calming music, possibly a floppy hat and sunglasses

You will want to use this sensory retreat often and throughout the day…not just when your child is in sensory overload. Be pro-active about it and use it as a place to re-group and help your sensory kiddo self-regulate. Use it between rides, anytime you are doing a lot of waiting, and any time your child seems to need it or request it!

SENSORY TOOLS

Once again…you have likely travelled by car or by plane and already have your sensory tools! Just be sure you bring them along to the amusement park. It may seem like extra work and a hassle, but you will be so happy you hauled it all with you ☺.

Here is a list of the essentials….

- Portable sensory retreat
- Oral sensory tools and Camelbak® water bottle
- Earplugs or noise cancelling headphones
- Floppy hat and/or sunglasses
- Compression clothing
- And lots and lots of bear hugs and deep pressure touch all day long. ☺

AMUSEMENT PARK FOOD AND DRINKS

If your child is sensitive to food dyes, additives and preservatives, or is on a GF/CF diet, then a restricted diet is required. The park will need to allow for you to bring in special foods for the restricted diet.

If your child is not on a restricted diet, please note that most, if not all, sensory kiddos are very sensitive to food dyes, preservatives, sugars, and are usually carb cravers. Even though the amusement park is often the time that children are given all sorts of treats, it is important to balance this and keep it limited. Focus on the protein rich foods and bring along snacks that are crunchy or chewy such as apples, carrot sticks, cheese sticks, fruit leather, etc. And try to stick to water as the drink of the day, unless you are buying milk…stay away from the rest of the sugary drinks.

The food and drinks that the child consumes during that day at the amusement park WILL make a difference in their mood, ability to self-regulate, and ability to cope with the sensory challenges at hand.

PUBLIC BATHROOMS

I can just hear it now…the dreaded HUGE public bathroom with VERY loud automatic flushing toilets and automatic hand dryers that sound like a plane taking off. And not just one…but 6-10 of each of these going on/off at different rates, unexpectedly! People rushing around in a hurry to get to the next ride, and sometimes screaming and crying babies on the changing table. I am in sensory overload just thinking about it. ☹

Be prepared. Don't just rush your child in there without the right tools…noise cancelling headphones or earplugs, if needed. Carry your child into the bathroom providing a nice deep pressure hug. Don't rush her around and get into a tizzy like the rest of the people in the bathroom.

If at all possible, use the COMPANION RESTROOM or the FAMILY RESTROOM. This will cut down on a ton of this unnecessary sensory input.

ENOUGH IS ENOUGH

Staying close to the amusement park can be your saving grace. Even though it may be a little more expensive to stay at a hotel on the grounds or very nearby, when your sensory kiddo has had enough…they have had enough. If you have more than one child with you, hopefully you also have an extra adult along with you. If so, then one parent can leave when your sensory kiddo is ready to go. Trying to push through is not the answer…it will only create a snowball effect, and the whole family will need a sensory retreat by the end of the day if you do so. ☺ Expect that you may need to leave early with your sensory kiddo.

9 WATER PARKS

ANOTHER MULTI-SENSORY EXPERIENCE

Now there is an off season for the water parks in Florida, but it still may be a little chilly if you do try to go in the off season. So for the most part, water parks are experienced in the summer only. My suggestion is to come early when they first open or at the end of the day. This can be very helpful in the overall experience.

I often rant and rave about how wonderful swimming is for a sensory kiddo, since it is an excellent way to get very powerful proprioception and also to develop body awareness and motor skills. The water park may be the exception to this rule. ☹

A water park can be a real challenge for a sensory child as it is like an amusement park and the beach and the pool all combined into one challenging sensory environment. Sensory kiddos, especially sensory avoiders, are just as content at a nice calm neighborhood pool. They will likely not participate too much at the water park. You may find yourself separated from the rest of the family spending time in the calm and relaxing "basic pool" while everyone else if off doing the waterslides. Even the kiddo pool area may be too much splashing and screaming.

Now for a sensory seeker, a water park may sound like a great place, but there may be a safety issue. Since the child may get into her "sensory tunnel", the next thing you know, she may have run off to the wave pool and jumped into the deep end. A child needs direct supervision everywhere at the water park.

THE RIDES

The tough part about the water park rides is that there usually is not a place for your belongings at the beginning of the ride. Typically there are lockers somewhere in the park instead. In this case, it is difficult to bring along some of your sensory tools while waiting in line. You cannot bring them on the ride due to the water factor, and there will not be a safe place to keep your belongings.

Water park rides are even more unpredictable than at an amusement park because, as we all know, on a water slide your body can get tossed and flipped in all directions, unlike when you are buckled into a basic amusement park ride. Also, usually at the end of a water ride there is the unexpected dump into a big pool of water, which can be very unpredictable as well. Even for the sensory seekers this can be a very challenging thing.

Then you have the wave pool…this can be wonderful, but also a disaster. The wave pool is big, unpredictable, and powerful. Even when your child plays near the shore of the waves it can be challenging, but also so tempting for the sensory seeker. Even if you bring your child out into the waves on a tube, be cautious and ready for the unexpected bump and flip of the tube from the people next to you going a little crazy. The wave pool seems to be such a popular and busy place all of the time.

THE SUN

The sun is draining and even more powerful when it reflects off of the water. Be sure your sensory kiddo has a floppy hat and polarized sunglasses with plenty of time in the shade and drinking a ton of water. This component is tough on all of us, but even more challenging for a child faced with sensory challenges.

SENSORY TOOLS

Here is a list of the essential tools for the water park…

- Putty swimmer's earplugs, not only for the sensation of the water, but to wear the entire time to cut down on the auditory input
- Swimming goggles or a swimmer's mask
- Oral sensory tools and a Camelbak® water bottle with water only
- Floppy hat and polarized sunglasses
- Portable sensory retreat

A PORTABLE SENSORY RETREAT

This was discussed in the previous chapter on amusement parks, so for the most part this information is repeated. But one of the essentials at the water park will need to be a stroller with a canopy or light weight blanket covering it for shade. The main components of the portable sensory retreat need to be:

- Cozy and squishy (lots of blankets and a stuffed animal or pillow)
- Use a blanket to cover the entire stroller to minimize all sensory input.
- Something weighted if possible, such as a weighted lap pad or blanket
- Fidget toy and possibly a vibrating toy or vibrating pillow
- Oral sensory tools
- Crunchy and chewy snacks
- Earplugs or noise-cancelling headphones, MP3 player with soft and calming music, possibly a floppy hat and sunglasses

You will want to use this sensory retreat often and throughout the day…not just when your child is in sensory overload. Be pro-active about it and use it as a place to re-group and help your sensory kiddo self-regulate. Use it between rides, anytime you are doing a lot of waiting, and whenever your child seems to need it or request it for a little down time.

THE KIDDO POOL

The kiddo pool may be your home away from home with your little sensory seeker. And for your sensory avoider, it may be good in small doses. I would strongly recommend goggles or a mask even at a very young age as well as swimmer's ear plugs. The feeling of the water splashing in the eyes and ears can be just the trigger to send your child into sensory overload. And we all know that the splashing is far from minimal at the water park in the kiddo pool.

THE LAZY RIVER AND STANDARD POOL

My guess is with your sensory avoider you will find yourself spending most of your time in the lazy river (most water parks have one) and the standard, regular ol' pool. It is best to expect this and be prepared for this, because setting your expectations too high will only be a big disappointment and even perhaps frustrating for a parent.

This is also a great place for your sensory seeker to spend time…it is your best option for organizing and regulating sensory input. Your sensory seeker will need this being in an environment where sensory input abounds in a very multi-sensory and chaotic fashion.

10 RESOURCES AND LINKS

In this chapter you will find valuable links, resources, and information from some of the most common and popular theme parks in the United States. You will also find a sample copy of a letter of explanation of hidden special needs. A complimentary copy of this letter is available to you at UnderstandingSPD.com.

NOTE: The information was obtain in 2011/2012 from the specified parks and may change over time in regards to the process, website links, and current programs offered.

Overall in my search for information and programs I must give thanks and recognition to the Walt Disney parks, as they promptly responded to my request and provided comprehensive information and tools to learn more about the programs offered for those with special needs. On the other hand, there were a number of theme parks I attempted to contact who never even responded to me and my request. I am including information on the businesses who indeed did reply to my request. As you will see Disney parks offer the most comprehensive programs out there for our children.

WALT DISNEY THEME PARKS

The information I gathered remains the same and is consistent across all Walt Disney Theme parks, including Disney Land and Disney World. Slight differences in wording may be found, but overall, the processes and programs offered are the same.

http://disneyworld.disney.go.com/guests-with-disabilities/

Disney parks offer the FASTPASS for those with special needs. This can be obtain at Guest Relations upon arrival.
The FASTPASS is free of charge and allows your family to access the shorter line at the rides where the FASTPASS service is available.

RIDER SWAP is another option available for those families who have children in the party too young to ride a specific ride and will need to wait with that child, and the adult guests can "swap" places in line so they do not have to wait in line twice.

TRANSPORTATION: There are buses, ferry boats, and monorails for getting from one park to another. Utilize these free services as often as possible since the Disney parks are very spread out. This will also allow for a nice dose of down time and calming sensory input for your child (and yourself!). ☺

Guests with food allergies or intolerances are allowed to bring food items into any Disney theme parks. Let the staff know at the security bag check that your child has a food allergy or intolerance.

Guest Assistance Card

The Guest Assistance Card is a tool provided at all four WALT DISNEY WORLD Resort Theme Parks to enhance the service we provide to our Guests. It was designed to alert our Cast about those Guests who may need additional assistance. The intent of these cards is to keep Guests from having to explain their service needs each time they visit an attraction.

The Guest Assistance Card is available to our Guests with non-apparent, special assistance needs. Depending on a Guest's need, this card may provide a variety of assistance such as allowing Guests to wait in a shaded area or providing admission to our attractions through auxiliary entrances, where applicable.

The intention of this card has never been to bypass attraction wait times.

A Guest with a specific need for assistance can request a Guest Assistance Card at any Theme Park Guest Relations location upon arrival. A doctor's note is not required. To accommodate the individual needs of our Guests, we ask that all Guests discuss their assistance requests with a Guest Relations Cast Member prior to the card being issued. The Guest Relations Cast Member will discuss the available service options with the Guest and provide written instructions for our Cast on the Guest Assistance Card. The Guest will be directed to present the Guest Assistance Card to the Greeter or first available Cast Member at the attraction and await further directions for their experience.
***Disney World Online Communications**

When your family arrives at guest relations, all you need to do is explain your situation briefly and present documentation if you desire (not required). If you don't want to disclose your exact medical condition, you are not required to do so. You just need to explain the type of accommodations that you need. Be sure your sensory kiddo comes along with you to Guest Services to obtain the card. This is required.

The Guest Assistance Card will also come in very handy if you would like to bring your "portable sensory retreat" (the stroller) with you while waiting in line. This is an option while waiting for some attractions.

BUSCH GARDENS AND SEA WORLD

http://seaworldparks.com/en/buschgardens-tampa/Park-Info/Special-Needs

http://seaworldparks.com/en/seaworld-sandiego/Park-Info/Special-Needs

Busch Gardens offers a ride accessibility program for guests with special needs. Go to Guest Relations upon arrival to the park to obtain the pass. Present the recommended letter of need if desired.

You then present the pass at each ride and will receive a Virtual Queue card to return in the current wait time to board the ride via the ADA accessible entrance.

WET 'N WILD

From the information I was sent, the only option you have for shorter lines is to purchase an Express Pass. Other than providing life jackets at no cost, I did not find any other free or really noteworthy resources for children with special needs at Wet 'N Wild.

SIX FLAGS THEME PARKS

The Six Flags website is a little complicated as it is one main website for over 10 Six Flags locations. Once you use the drop down menu on the right to access the desired location, you can then search for Guest Relations. I was unable to locate any specific pages or information for special needs on the main page. Here is a sample link for one of the locations in California.

Magic Mountain

http://www.sixflags.com/magicMountain/info/ guestrelations.aspx

GUESTS WITH DISABILITIES

The following information was found on the website in reference to the Magic Mountain location. Each separate location has different information and protocols. I know, confusing.

For information on services offered to guests with disabilities, please visit Guest Relations located in Six Flags Plaza, where representatives will be pleased to help personalize your visit. Pick up our "Guest with Disabilities Guide," a handout that provides detailed information on accessibility of rides, shows, games, shops and restaurants.

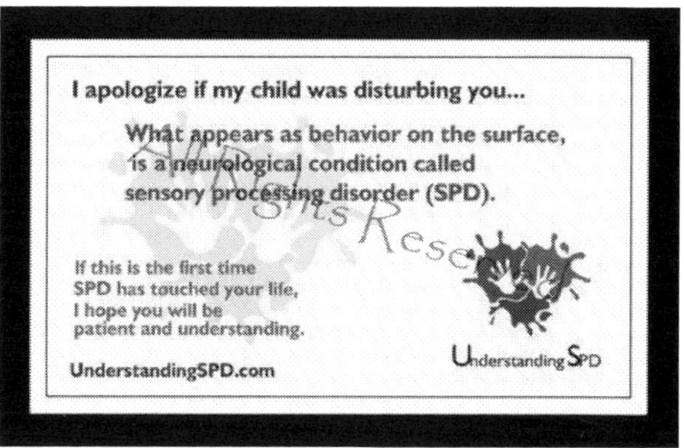

These sensory awareness cards are available for purchase at **UnderstandingSPD.com** for a small fee and may come in very handy on your vacation. The actual cards are bright and colorful, on a glossy and sturdy pocket size card. They are sold in packs of 25 and are a nice little tool and shield of armor for those moments when someone gives you "the glare" or the look of disapproval when your child is in sensory overload or is having a meltdown moment or perhaps a fight or flight episode. SPD is tough to explain since it is a "hidden disability" and your child will look typical to the average bear.

Just remain calm and simply hand the lovely person a card and walk away. ☺

This sample letter is available to print out complimentary at **UnderstandingSPD.com.**

UnderstandingSPD.com

Sensory Solutions, PLLC   Angie Voss, OTR/L

Hidden Disability Awareness and Letter of Explanation
Special Needs and Accommodations
Sensory Processing Disorder (SPD)

Sensory Processing Disorder (SPD) is a neurological condition in which the brain and nervous system have difficulty processing sensory information from one or all of the senses. This may involve the well known senses, but also the vestibular and proprioceptive senses. These sensory processing difficulties impact a child's ability to tolerate and accept sensory input in the environment on a constant basis. A child may seek out sensory input or avoid it, or a combination of the two. Theme parks/amusement parks offer significant amounts of new and challenging multi-sensory input.

Areas which will likely be a challenge and present difficulty during our visit include:

- Ability to wait in lines
- Tolerating multi-sensory input such as loud and unexpected sounds, bright, colorful and moving objects, etc
- Social interactions and the ability to communicate with new people
- Using public restrooms
- Eating in a large cafeteria type restaurant
- Bumping into and walking in close proximity to others
- Safety and judgment, impulsivity
- New experiences and rides

In order for my child to have the best experience possible and to maximize safety, it is strongly recommended and requested that special consideration be made for my child with sensory processing disorder and our family. Thank you so much for your understanding.

For Further Information Visit: UnderstandingSPD.com

For further information, sensory blog posts, free sensory forms and resources please visit:
UnderstandingSPD.com

Additional titles by Angie Voss, OTR/L

~ *Understanding Your Child's Sensory Signals*

~ *Your Essential Guide to Understanding Sensory Processing Disorder*

Made in the USA
Lexington, KY
17 May 2012